Copyright 2023
Little WooWoo Publishing
All rights reserved

No portion of this book may be reproduced
in any form without permission from the publisher
except as permitted by copyright law.

A Book of Many Interesting Dinosaurs....

(So many differences, but all are Dinosaurs!)

By
Newton E. White

As you may or may not know, there are many dinosaurs that have lived, or might live around the world, at school or even in your house or home. They are all different....

A Styracosaurus might be very young

...or a little older

A Stegosaurus can be quite bulky...

Others can be quite petite

Some Pterodactyl's are blue...

....Others might be yellow

Some Diplodocuses are very studious

Others can be very sporty

Some Ankylosaurus love vegetables

Others much prefer cake!

Some T-Rex like to climb...

Others really like to dig

Some Spinosaurus's like to play in groups

Others like to play alone

Some dinosaurs enjoy drinking orange juice...

Others prefer to drink water

Some dinosaurs like to ride bicycles...

Others like to travel by bus!

Some Triceratops like to play on a tablet

Others prefer to listen to some tunes

Some dinosaurs love the sun

Others quite like playing in the rain!

Some dinosaurs have pet dogs....

And some dinosaurs have pet cats (or cats have pet dinosaurs?!)

But.........no dinosaur wants to be lonely

It doesn't matter what dinosaurs look like, what they like to do, or how different they are. Give them a smile as every dinosaur can be friends....

Which dinosaur would you be?

The End

www.ingramcontent.com/pod-product-compliance
Lightning Source LLC
Chambersburg PA
CBHW051322110526
44590CB00031B/4442